D0948823

SETH ROLLINS:
THE ARCHITECT

Fly!
An Imprint of Abdo Zoom
abdobooks.com

KENNY ABDO

abdobooks.com

Published by Abdo Zoom, a division of ABDO, P.O. Box 398166, Minneapolis, Minnesota 55439. Copyright © 2020 by Abdo Consulting Group, Inc. International copyrights reserved in all countries. No part of this book may be reproduced in any form without written permission from the publisher. Fly!™ is a trademark and logo of Abdo Zoom.

Printed in the United States of America, North Mankato, Minnesota.
052019
092019

THIS BOOK CONTAINS RECYCLED MATERIALS

Photo Credits: Alamy, AllWrestlingSuperstars.com, Seth Poppel/Yearbook Library, Shutterstock, The Black & The Brave Wrestling Academy, Vlad, © Vlad p.cover, © Miguel Discart p4, p5, p8, p12, p14, p16 / CC BY-SA 2.0, © Julie Ahn p7 / CC BY-SA 2.0, © Megan Elice Meadows p13 / CC BY-SA 2.0
Production Contributors: Kenny Abdo, Jennie Forsberg, Grace Hansen
Design Contributors: Dorothy Toth, Neil Klinepier

Library of Congress Control Number: 2018963797

Publisher's Cataloging-in-Publication Data

Names: Abdo, Kenny, author.
Title: Seth Rollins: the architect / by Kenny Abdo.
Other title: The architect
Description: Minneapolis, Minnesota : Abdo Zoom, 2020 | Series: Wrestling biographies set 2 | Includes online resources and index.
Identifiers: ISBN 9781532127557 (lib. bdg.) | ISBN 9781532128530 (ebook) | ISBN 9781532129025 (Read-to-me ebook)
Subjects: LCSH: Rollins, Seth (Colby Lopez)--Juvenile literature. | Wrestlers--United States--Biography--Juvenile literature. | World Wrestling Entertainment Studios--Juvenile literature.
Classification: DDC 796.812092 [B]--dc23

TABLE OF CONTENTS

Seth Rollins 4

Early Years 6

WWE 10

Legacy 18

Glossary 22

Online Resources 23

Index 24

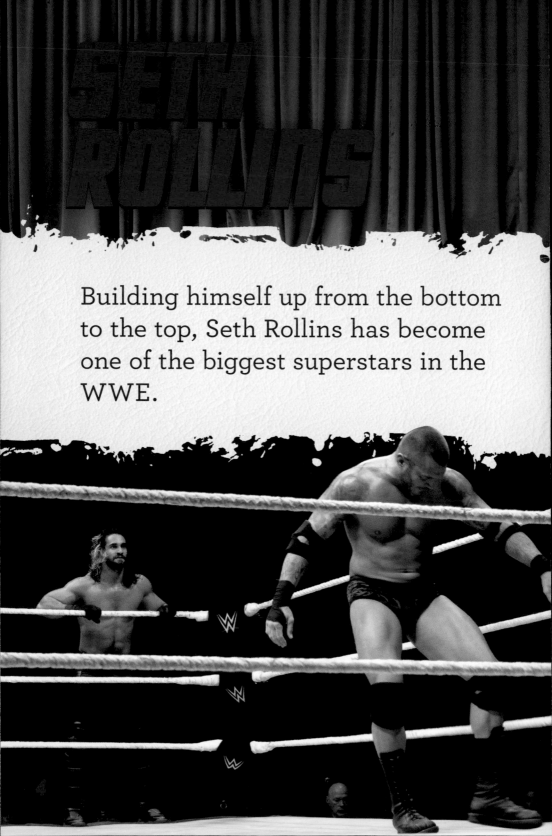

SETH ROLLINS

Building himself up from the bottom to the top, Seth Rollins has become one of the biggest superstars in the WWE.

Rollins first dominated the ring as part of the infamous team The Shield. Then he became even more unstoppable when he went solo.

Colby Lopez was born in Buffalo, Iowa, in 1986.

Lopez made his **debut** at 17 in a Scott County Wrestling (SCW) event. He moved to the Ring of Honor (ROH) in 2007. He fought as Tyler Black and won the ROH World **Championship** in 2010.

Lopez signed with WWE **NXT** in 2010 as Seth Rollins. He went on to become the first ever NXT champion.

Rollins made his WWE **debut** as a member of The Shield, a team made up of Dean Ambrose and Roman Reigns, in 2012. He left the team in 2014 after **betraying** them in the ring.

Rollins won his first **WWE Championship** at Wrestlemania 31. At **SummerSlam** 2017, Rollins reunited with Ambrose. Together, they claimed the Raw Tag Team **titles**.

Rollins became a Grand Slam Champion at WrestleMania 34. There, he won the Intercontinental **title**.

Rollins won the 2019 **Royal Rumble** Match by eliminating Braun Strowman. That gave him a chance to take the Universal **Championship title** away from Brock Lesner at WrestleMania 35!

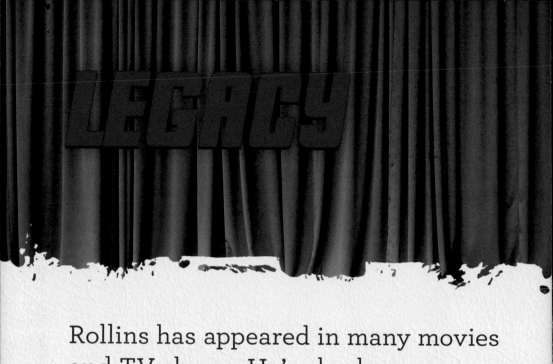

Rollins has appeared in many movies and TV shows. He's also been a playable character in every WWE video game since 2013.

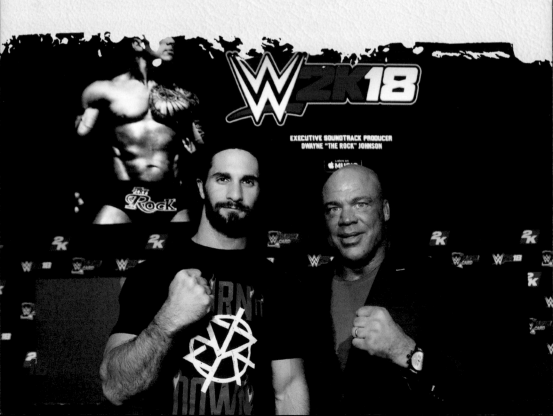

Rollins opened his own wrestling school with Marek Brave in Illinois. It is called The Black & The Brave Wrestling Academy. There, they train up-and-coming fighters to reach for the top!

GLOSSARY

betray – to turn against, lie to, or hurt.

championship – a game, match, or race held to find a first-place winner.

debut – to appear for the first time.

NXT – WWE's developmental brand. WWE uses NXT to help wrestlers learn and grow before bringing them to the main roster.

Royal Rumble – a major WWE show held every year in January.

SummerSlam – a major WWE show held every year in August.

title – the position of being the best in that division.

WWE Championship – the top prize in WWE.

ONLINE RESOURCES

Booklinks
NONFICTION NETWORK
FREE! ONLINE NONFICTION RESOURCES

To learn more about Seth Rollins, please visit **abdobooklinks.com** or scan this QR code. These links are routinely monitored and updated to provide the most current information available.

INDEX

Ambrose, Dean 11, 12

Black & The Brave Wrestling Academy, The 21

Brave, Marek 21

Iowa 6

Lesner, Brock 16

NXT 9

Reigns, Roman 11

Ring of Honor (ROH) 7

Scott County Wrestling (SCW) 7

Shield, The (team) 5, 11

Strowman, Braun 16

SummerSlam 12

WrestleMania 12, 15, 16

WWE 4, 9, 11, 12, 18